SOUTINE

SOUTINE

by Marcellin Castaing and Jean Leymarie

---

59 reproductions with 34 in color

HARRY N. ABRAMS, INC. · PUBLISHERS
NEW YORK, N.Y.

CONTENTS

INTRODUCTION

It has become established practice to bury painting under bushels of literature, notwithstanding the fact that painting is an art primarily concerned with the sensibilities, around which, indeed, it is centered. By comparison with the feelings inspired by a painting, all explanation is futile. Theories, schools, and periods have their uses, but only for purposes of demonstration and classification in a history of art. When we get to the heart of the matter, considerations of space and time, schools and systems no longer count: only the individual and his work concern us. But individuality is a rare thing, which we carry within us. It provides its own explanation without outside aids, and the conscious search for individuality leads only to singularity, to eccentricity, the caricature of individuality. A painting is a creation; the painter's emotions and imagination together give him the power to bring life to all he sees. From that moment on he has abolished time. Without life everything must perish and be lost. He does away with space, too, and consequently eliminates the conception of progress in art and, with it, the hierarchy of major works. By its humanity, Titian's portrait of Charles the Fifth reaches out to meet the Man with Pipe, *one of Van Gogh's self-portraits. Schools fade away and are replaced by individuals. What is left of the Impressionist school, one of the most widely represented? Men like Monet, Sisley, or Pissarro? What would Divisionism be without Seurat, or Cubism without Picasso? As for theories, they must be studied for their own sake, then left aside. They have given rise to a disorderly, contradictory literature in which painting is relegated to a place of secondary importance; they disappear of their own accord when faced with the ultimate mystery of the work itself.*

But what is this power to give life, the power that makes the individual? Definitions of painting provide the answer, and they are all contained in those of Fromentin and Delacroix. The former wrote: " Painting is nothing more than the art of expressing the invisible through the visible," and the latter: " Realism is the most real *expression of objects by means of their imitation in painting." Though the terms used are different, the meaning is the same, and a whole succession of examples springs to mind. Ingres, whose formal perfection caused men to deny instinct and hesitate before passing judgment, would not be the complete painter esteemed as he is now, if he had only left* The Apotheosis of Homer, *whatever its merits; but he also put all the self-sufficiency of his contemporary bourgeois into the portrait of* Monsieur Bertin *and made it a permanent reality, just as El Greco made the two figures at the foot of the Cross the complete expression of faith and turned them into symbols of grandeur and spirituality. Rem-*

brandt's Jewish Bride *is a monument of tenderness. Faced with the "inner strength"—to borrow Delacroix's expression—of Courbet's* Studio Model, *Manet's* Olympia *takes its place as a pretty picture. The great landscape painters are creators of atmosphere. In his* Trees in Spring, *Pissarro conveyed the tremors of nature renewing itself. There in all their variety we have Fromentin's "invisible" or Delacroix's "most real realism," the life's breath of painting. In great works there are always mysterious turmoils lying behind the mere diversity of techniques. Bonnard drew the practical conclusion from this: "One can study nature, dissect and analyze and balance it, without making paintings."*

Small or great, whatever their position, all painters aspire to this intangible content beyond the surface of the painting, for fear of remaining limited to appearances; they know that a painter who appeals only to the senses is nothing more than clever with his hands, and is not fulfilling his real task. Many highly reputed masterpieces astonish, but do not move us. What the painter transmits to us is first of all his emotion, starting from the object that provided the original stimulus. After that we are at liberty to ask how he did it, once the result is achieved. Defeat comes when one is limited to realism, which is the direct opposite of art. In fact, it hides reality from us.

As always, poetry has the last word. It dominates the whole field. Everything already said here leads back to poetry. Forms are linked to it in order to live. As Baudelaire said, it is "the ultimate reason for art," which demonstrates the futility of works lacking the spark of poetry. But where does the poet stand in all this? Poetry is not a result to be presented: it is rather a fountainhead, the virgin spring of the predestined.

All these are essential truths, but too often they are left dormant. It took a great name like Soutine to reawaken them without apparent effort.

Therefore I do not intend to embark on abstruse, purposeless discussions. This will be my point of departure for talking about Soutine. To speak of Soutine is to speak of painting. My aim is to place him among his own kind: when one goes beyond the threshold of mere talent, the main interest lies in showing what distinguishes geniuses from each other, by pinning down their individuality. To define Soutine is above all to define a total liberty that was unknown before him. He follows none of the intentions or preconceptions that one feels sometimes hampered the greatest, at times even Cézanne. He knows nothing of the didactic attitude that can break or divert one's impetus. He delivers us from fear of the snares of intellectualism. "A great painter thinks with his brushes in his hand." Baudelaire's maxim coincides impressively with Balzac's: "A great painter should only meditate when he has his brushes in his hand." And indeed Soutine, the instinctive, inspired painter, must be judged on this essential, spiritual plane, for this is his rightful place.

Thus freed from the customary obstacles, he pursued his effort right to its ultimate consequences with only one thought in mind: to extract the reality from people and things. This determination was so great that sometimes he would cut around the part of a painting in which he felt he had captured this reality. The rest was waste: he kept only a fragment, but that fragment contained the miracle. This austere approach to his work is significant and it is important

Chère Madame Castaing

Venez poser cet après midi
à 2 heures avec une robe
blanche sans manches
car je n'irai pas aujourd'hui
chez madame Saxe de ne vous
je suis dégoûté
faire.

Cordialement

Soutine.

to stress it from the outset if we are to understand Soutine, who demanded this miracle from every canvas he painted and was implacable toward anything that distracted him. One day he was painting a woman lying reading on a couch. The particular inspiration—a gesture, an attitude, a glance—he longed for and would seize upon, would not come. Meanwhile he set to work on the dress, which became more and more important and sumptuous, and with his natural virtuosity he made it into an astonishing piece of work. As usual the pose he had insisted on was tyrannical and lasted until the moment when the woman, at the limit of her endurance, began to stare at the book as if it were an instrument of torture. This was the moment that inspired the painter and he grasped for it, but eliminated the dress in case people might look at it instead of at the essential part, which for him was elsewhere. The painter's career is inseparable from this intransigence, and is punctuated with destruction all along the line. He has been called a saint of painting. I am happy to quote the painter-to-painter judgment of one of his friends: " We sometimes worked together. It was by adoring reality that he created his immense pictorial universe. I have seen him spend weeks searching for a certain light, a certain motif, and once he found it he never stopped halfway in his efforts, he was never content with facile effects. I believe in the exemplary value of his artistic conscience."

He lived in constant expectation of the shock produced by model or theme, and when he discovered them he was transformed; he would shut himself away from all outside contacts, for he had become a man possessed, and it is thanks to this absolute communion with people and things that we can know them now. We know that no two whites are quite the same. The white of the Communicant is not the same as the white of the Choirboy, and that white is not the same as that of the Pastrycook or the Valet. His renowned reds follow all the overtones of their own lives. We often pass in front of a display of poultry and all we see is a display of poultry. But these half-open beaks and glassy eyes, the deathly pale bodies with the two stumps of wings still brandishing great black feathers, the claws desperately clutching at empty space, the whole hung by the neck from a hook, constitute a drama that Soutine reveals to us. Creation comes to the aid of our own incapacities. Soutine lays bare the permanent, hidden side of physical signs. This is why such truths often seem strange in the eyes of a surprised public that does not recognize its own life. But this is true of all the arts.

So, Soutine was pursuing the inaccessible. This demand dominated him, and in this fusion of matter and life, which is the great temptation of the initiated, it was his very nature that expressed itself. Tormented, proud, ambitious for his work, his life as a painter was a hectic but continuous advance toward the realization of the inner order that gives weight to inspired works, and this he found in Rembrandt. Exalting in his mastery, he arrived at this equilibrium and his cycle was completed.

In short, when one agrees about Soutine one agrees about painting. With his deep, creative color he penetrates to the heart of things: indeed, starting with the object and avoiding repetition of forms, " to grasp the intangible" (if we may use Edgar Allan Poe's phrase), is the great difficulty of painting and the reason for its existence. It is also the last word in the argument about abstract and informal.

Hanging Fowl (Private collection)

Soutine's technique corresponded to his genius. He attacked directly with color and conjured up form and life. A glance, a touch. There is no stroke in his work that is not inspired and instinctively well placed. Violent or refined, never static, they keep the freshness of the first moment and do not tire the canvas. Human richness through richness of matter: few painters can have been as rich as he. He drew all the substance from colors and penetrated into their mysterious life. He realized the hope of Cézanne: "When color is rich, form is at its plenitude," and perhaps also the prophecy of his elder, a visionary like himself, Van Gogh: "The painter of the future is a colorist the likes of which has yet to be seen."

It is a difficult task to find the man behind the artist. He has to be extricated from the mounds of legend and literature, as I have just done for Soutine the painter. Jewish, Russian, and a genius: this combination resulted in a personality which was strange, it must be admitted, but strong and basically very engaging. Nothing was simple. Contradictions and whims were the stuff of his life. But he had one inviolable rule: he never mentioned a living painter. He might be miles away, outside time, and suddenly he would come back to earth and concentrate on some minute detail whose interest or importance was apparent to him alone. There was always a secret, complicated side to the reasons for his actions. In this way the boxing matches he followed assiduously afforded him a visual emotion that was linked in his mind with his cult of Grecian statuary. I mention this as an example of the obscure ramifications of a mind always in movement. There were two Soutines, the Soutine of painting and the Soutine of idleness. The one was as exaggerated as the other. Once his canvases were finished he would tear them up or hide them. I have spoken of the innumerable works he destroyed. He rejected the canvases of his Céret period and took an almost voluptuous delight in seeing them disappear. His hiding places occasioned childish ruses and roundabout procedures. Exposure (his word) of his work was painful for him. He wanted no exhibitions during his lifetime. He was even more firmly opposed to frames, hanging on walls, and often even signatures. On the other hand, he took almost maniacal care over the choice of canvas and colors and the cleanliness of his brushes. And he was right, for his paintings age well. It was in this complex setting that we had the privilege of seeing them, and seeing him, for the first time. No mean right, this. The session took place in accordance with an unvarying ritual. He was on the watch for our first movement, the good one, he said. One had to pronounce the expected word and, depending on the case, this could lead to catastrophes or apotheoses. Soutine did not know what a controlled reaction was. One day he had finished a canvas and was fidgeting anxiously in front of it. The canvas was a success and attractive, but the range of colors struck me as unusual for him. I automatically mentioned Renoir, whereupon he immediately tore up the painting—not because he despised Renoir, but because he wanted to resemble himself and no one else. In periods of calm, whose lengths were impossible to predict, he liked to improve himself. Balzac was his man. One day I found him sunk in the Michelet from our library. This history fascinated him and he often returned to it. He was very attached to our house at Lèves, and came for long stays that became a tradition lasting twenty years. He painted many of his finest works there. He spent a lot of time in museums. Once he left suddenly for Amsterdam and returned no less suddenly: he had seen The Jewish

Chere Madame Castaing,

Je vous prie venez
me voir cet après-
midi, j'ai abso-
lument besoin
vous parler au sujet que
de mon exposition
j'ai vu hier
Je suis complètement
découragé cordialement
Soutine

Bride. *Often we went with him, to our great profit, to The Louvre. He would go into ecstasies over the despairing (again, his word) quality of certain mediums, but there was nothing to rival his emotion before things human. He surprised us with the accuracy, in all their spontaneity, of his remarks. He went straight to some detail, of capital importance, he would say, that would otherwise have passed unnoticed, an open mouth, the hand of a child on its mother's breast, the sharpness or sweetness of a gaze, the reality of an attitude taken unawares. Sometimes, in some works, there is a miraculous point in which all the painter's sensibility is concentrated, and from that point there radiates the magic that gives meaning to the entire painting: for instance, a face that makes one forget the rest. This is a disconcerting moment, when genius goes beyond the limits of its own laws.*

The phenomenon of the human is a need: its action is deep and universal. It is banal to say that the Mona Lisa was chosen for her historic journey because of her smile, but this gives yet another illustration of what I have been trying to say, and of the vital preoccupation of Soutine.

The lesson of our outings was always the same and I shall give it as a conclusion. Familiarity with the masterpieces of museums, and attentive, selective visits to the big retrospective shows that have become one of the attractions of Paris, are the best methods to avoid being duped by the false audacities aimed at the usual victims of " works of art."

M. CASTAING

House and Garden at Lèves

Modigliani. *Portrait of Soutine* (Staatliche Kunstsammlungen, Stuttgart)

Soutine was already a legend during his lifetime, but the mystery that surrounds him still remains intact, distorted only by a few absurd anecdotes. Those exhibitions attempted since his death have so far given only incomplete or false pictures of his art. Too many inconsistent or downright suspect canvases—including the youthful experiments he was later to disown—mask the true grandeur of a body of work whose crowning fulfillment and finest gems are still unknown. These are jealously guarded by collectors who vow a fervent, exclusive cult to their idol and will not tolerate the slightest shadow of doubt concerning his genius. In addition to the absolutely unpublished drawings, nineteen of the thirty-four paintings chosen for color reproduction here come from one of the two, or maybe three, virtually secret collections that contain Soutine's best work: there can be no doubt that they constitute an exceptional revelation, and this is the justification for the present volume, in which the quality of the illustrations permits a new approach to one of the strangest and most arresting geniuses of our times.

Soutine's personality escapes us, and in the absence of the full-scale retrospective for which the time now seems ripe, even the chronology of his work has not yet been established. The most important part, the essential concerning this painter who ranks among the greatest, has been vigorously outlined here by the privileged witness, Marcellin Castaing. After his short but decisive presentation, what I have to say, which is of necessity completely provisional, runs the risk of appearing secondary or hazardous.

The tenth in a wretchedly poor Jewish family of eleven children, Chaim Soutine was born in 1893 in the little Lithuanian village of Smilovichi, on the banks of the Berezina. A minority enclave socially and psychologically different from the western ghetto, the Jewish community in the Slavic countries, with its primitive, autonomous structure, the *shtetl*, often formed a center of cultural, if not artistic life around the synagogue. But not in this obscure hamlet, where there was no decoration in the prayer house and Soutine knew nothing of the patriarchal warmth and mystical poetry evoked by Chagall in his memories of Vitebsk. Soutine knew only hunger, blows, humiliation, and oppressive promiscuity in an environment from which he felt himself cut off and against which he revolted, though the wounds it left him were never to heal. His father, a coarse, uneducated man, a poor country tailor, wanted his son to become a cobbler, but who could foresee his inexplicable fate? How was it that in this hidden backwater, without ancestors, he carried in his blood not only the torments of his race, but also the irrepressible demon of painting? He used to like telling that, conscious of his destiny, he was fascinated by the glints of sunlight above his cradle before he could talk. When he was seven he stole his mother's kitchen knife to buy colored crayons. He was punished for this by two days of imprisonment in a dank closet in the cellar. He was poor at his schoolwork, and his difficult nature and unstable character led to his expulsion from school. He wandered around cottages and barns and sought refuge in the immense forest that surrounded the village, where he felt its terrifying magic. He drew human faces on walls with charcoal, an incomprehensible, scandalous vocation in the eyes of his

associates. He was cruelly beaten by the family of the Rabbi, whose portrait—oh offense and sacrilege—he had dared to draw.

He ran away to the nearby city of Minsk, the capital of White Russia, where he attended classes in drawing; he then moved on to Vilna, where he frequented the school of art and met up with his friends, Kikoine and Kremègne, who were to precede him to Paris. Barely adolescent, without resources, already scarred by life, wild and frank, he faced up to the town, with its turpitudes and temptations and provincial narrowness. The physical ills and Dostoevskian obsessions that were later to torment him can be traced back to this baneful stay in Vilna, filled with sexual frustration and social conflict. He arrived in Paris in his twentieth year, when the modern revolution in the plastic arts was at its height. Before even looking for a room he rushed to The Louvre. " So it was that one morning, in the soft light of the Ile-de-France," writes Waldemar George, his first commentator, " I saw an unknown young man with a low brow and a shifty gaze standing in front of the *Funeral at Ornans*. He moved on, hugging the walls. He seemed possessed by fear. Whenever anyone approached him he would move away. He looked at the works of masters of the past in the same way a believer gazes on holy images. I was curious, and followed him through the rooms of the museum. A few hours later, apparently satiated, he made for the way out, stopped in front of Ingres's *La Source*, then went downstairs to the cloakroom and took out a suitcase that no doubt contained his possessions. I got to know him two or three years later. It was Chaim Soutine."

The sudden appearance in the middle of the Paris school of these Jewish painters from the boundaries of the East, artists with no figurative tradition behind them, bursting with burning visions contained for ages, is characteristic of the beginning of our century, one of those phenomena that can never be repeated. The greatest among these newcomers were to assimilate everything and at the same time bring forth everything they bore within them; these riches burst out in a favorable atmosphere of creation and freedom. Much has been said about their ethnic or religious attachments. In fact, as Manès Sperber remarked: " They aimed at integrating themselves into art, not integrating art into their Judaism. Though Chaim Soutine remained the poor child of the *shtetl* right to his premature end, he was never the *shtetl's* painter in any way. He was the lone night traveler who meets only the dead: Rembrandt, Goya, Van Gogh." Only an exile from the farthest point in space and time could have sensed better in Old Masters than in contemporary examples the live fountainheads of painting and the brotherhood of its acolytes.

For a while Soutine strayed into the Beaux-Arts, in Cormon's class, where Lautrec and Van Gogh had passed before. Then, cured of his academic illusions, he pitched camp in Impasse Dantzig, in the great collective community of international bohemia, La Ruche, the famous rotunda off which studios opened like the cells of a honeycomb. Besides Kikoine and Kremègne, he found many compatriots there, in particular Marc Chagall, who was already in full possession of his style and whose intense early canvases Soutine saw. While the Bateau-Lavoir in Montmartre, another shrine of modern art, was the laboratory of form, La Ruche in Montparnasse tended more toward color, with Chagall and the Eastern school, Léger and Delaunay.

At the beginning of the First World War, after enlisting in the work brigades, which rejected him because of the state of his health, Soutine moved to Cité Falguière, not far from La Ruche, which he still haunted like his own sad, worried ghost. Cité Falguière was mainly occupied by sculptors, many of Russian origin. He shared a room with Miestchaninoff, who gave him great encouragement. In 1915 his fellow Lithuanian, Lipchitz, introduced him to Modigliani, who had a neighboring studio. With his open, generous nature and acute perception, capable of admiring Utrillo *and* Picasso, Modigliani immediately sensed the genius of Soutine beneath the rough-hewn surface. A strange, fruitful friendship grew up between these two, apparently so dissimilar men, the aristocratic, exuberant, cultivated Italian and the backward, wild, introverted Slav, one a virtuoso of line and the other possessed by color. But both were prototypes of the *peintre maudit*, and shared a fateful sense of human existence and its vulnerability. In 1917 Modigliani drew four majestic portraits of his as yet unknown young friend, prostrated in his dreams and solitude. His heavy, slanted eyes seem turned inward, while his admirable hands, soft and relaxed, stand out in the foreground on his stiff knees. "Refinement shows in the fingers," as Courbet said. Thanks to the support and understanding of his already famous elder, Soutine became conscious of himself and painted at that time his one and only self-portrait (Collection Henry Pearlman, New York) in a body of work that sprang out whole, like a burning confession.

Soutine destroyed much of his work, and little is left of his first steps. Around 1915 he painted a few desolate views of Cité Falguière with its sheds of uneven planks and its puny trees, and in 1916, a series of still lifes showing his kitchen table and his starvation-level pittance. For example: *Still Life with Soup Tureen* (Collection Ralph F. Colin, New York), *Still Life with Bottle* (Collection Pierre Lévy, Troyes), and above all, with the poignant strength and simplification that reveal his temperament, *Still Life with Herrings* (Collection Katia Granoff, Paris). The Dutch Old Masters had often treated the dish of herrings, the meal of the poor, which Van Gogh, too, had painted three times in Paris and once in Arles. In those hard times Soutine had often to make do with a skinny herring on a slice of bread, as he had to in Vilna, and took up the theme in his turn, in a livid scale of grays and browns on a black ground. Three herrings lie pathetically on a plate, their mouths open and their eyes popping out. Soutine adds cruelly expressive detail, thus increasing the drama of the pictorial content. As described by Charles Sterling, "Two iron forks, these bistro forks that bend and ring false, converge on the fish like two hands, thin, greedy, terrifying—the very claws of poverty."

In these stiffly composed still lifes viewed from above there is a preoccupation with form and line untypical of Soutine, who was soon to seize on his true element, sinuous, flowing touches of color; he accepted the traditional themes of painting—landscapes, portraits, still lifes—and reshaped them to fit his own disquiet. Depending on the necessity of the moment, one or other of these types was always to be dominant in his output. At the insistence of Kremègne and Modigliani, the latter's dealer, the Polish poet Leopold Zborowski, a curious figure living between business and bohemia, became Soutine's dealer too, but found difficulty in placing his canvases, even at low prices. In 1918, following Modigliani who was to stay there until spring 1919,

Pastrycook (Collection Mme Jean Walter, Paris)

Soutine discovered Provence, around Nice. The shock of his first contact with the Mediterranean, always impressive for a painter from the North, precipitated his development.

From 1919 to 1922 Soutine lived away from Paris and its post-war euphoria, and in solitude and anguish underwent a crucial transformation. He took refuge in Céret, in the East Pyrenees, and Cagnes, in the Alpes Maritimes, going from one to the other in a mysterious to-and-fro. Céret, a small town clustered in a mountainous setting, has been called " the Mecca of Cubism " by André Salmon, because of the heroic stays there of Picasso, Braque, and Juan Gris between 1911 and 1913. Cagnes, near Nice, the paradise garden where Renoir died in December 1919, had kept its old town perched on a feudal rock. It was there, in January 1920, that Soutine learned of the death of Modigliani and the suicide of his young mistress, an event which threw a shadow over the wild years of Montparnasse. The death of perhaps the only person he ever knew intimately, the man who had upheld him with his absolute confidence (Modigliani's last words are supposed to have saluted and recommended Soutine's genius), stirred up the inner storm that was then shaking him. His stomach was often empty, for the subsidies he received were often barely enough to buy paints, and in a few months he accumulated over two hundred frenzied canvases, many of which, true to type, were later to be destroyed. Gathered together by Zborowski, these paintings were discovered in Paris at the end of 1922 by the famous American collector, Dr. Albert C. Barnes, who, to the general stupefaction of artistic circles, immediately bought them on a massive scale.

In his longing for the absolute, Soutine rejected this stormy period, which he considered an eruption overloaded with dross, summary and chaotic. Today's taste for Expressionist violence and convulsive, tortured matter, leads us back to these canvases, out of a curiosity that is perhaps untimely. The Céret landscapes seem shaken by an earthquake that dislocates foundations to lay bare the substance. Trees, fields, houses, mixed and interlocking, rear up burning creepers (Collection Henry Pearlman, New York) or bound tumultuously to the right (Kunstmuseum, Lucerne), sometimes colliding with the chains of mountains that shut off the horizon. This oppressive surge covers the entire canvas, leaving little or no room for the sky. The inextricably thick, complex mass of pigments, greens, browns, yellows, in tightly packed half tones, impossible to reproduce, is like a flow of lava, a melting-pot of jewels. Though they are swept along by the same tornado of passion, there is a difference of rhythm between the harsh, knotted, compact views of Roussillon, pierced with tawny, glowing light, and those of Provence, softer and more curving, in which, despite the storm, one senses the tang of the sea and the breathing space of blue sky. One of the motifs most characteristic of Cagnes is *Red Stair, Le Piolet* (Collection Katia Granoff, Paris), a twisting, brick-paved street lined with tumble-down houses, that climbs up to the old castle. The human figure, which had always obsessed Soutine, underwent the same cataclysmic distortions before reaching its total truth, probed in depth and stripped of all masks. Toward the end of his stay, in 1922, when his color was beginning to settle and distill its chemistry, out of infinite variations of shades of a single tone sprang the first masterpiece, the *Woman in Red* (Collection Dr. and Mrs. Harry Bakwin, New York), majestic beneath

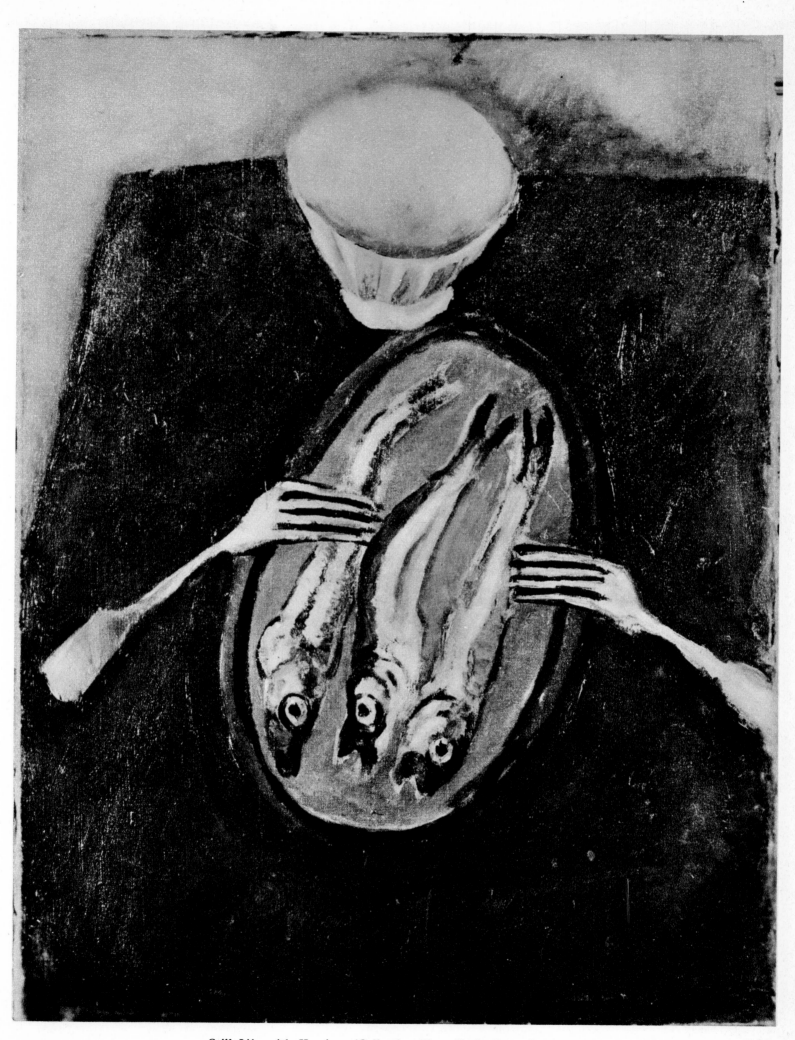

Still Life with Herrings (Collection Mme Katia Granoff, Paris)

her gigantic hat, or the touching *Pastrycook* (Collection Mme Jean Walter, Paris) who twists a scarlet kerchief against velvety whites, which was the first of his paintings to attract Dr. Barnes' attention and suddenly touch off Soutine's fame. As Paul Guillaume himself said: " One day I had gone to see a Modigliani in a painter's house, and in a corner of the studio I noticed a work that immediately filled me with enthusiasm. It was a Soutine, and it showed a pastrycook, an unprecedented pastrycook, fascinating, real, truculent, afflicted with an immense, superb ear, unexpected but absolutely right: a masterpiece. I bought it. Dr. Barnes saw it in my house. ' But it's a peach!' he cried. The spontaneous pleasure he experienced with this canvas was enough to decide Soutine's sudden turn of good fortune, and make him overnight into a well-known painter sought after by collectors, no longer a man to laugh at—a hero in Montparnasse."

This unforeseen success marks the end of his formative period. An instinctive painter, Soutine fought less to conquer his style than to control his inner tumult. After a red-hot gestation period, the Céret paroxysm proved to have been indispensable for Soutine's deliverance and fulfillment. It was also the crest of the wave that had started with Van Gogh in Saint-Rémy. As we know, Soutine became increasingly violent in his denials of this obsessive filiation. André Masson, who was also at Céret in 1919, tells how one day he incurred the Lithuanian's rage by mentioning the painter of the *Sunflowers*. " Taking a chance, in an attempt to calm him down, I asked him which painter he did like. Without hesitation he replied ' Rouault.'" With Rouault, Nolde, and Kokoschka, Soutine belongs to the dramatic dynasty of modern Expressionism founded by Van Gogh. But each of these two great recluses, Soutine and Rouault, who never knew each other, remains an irreducible case; the affinities between the two depend exclusively on the climate of the times. They were opposed in approach and conception, and converged only insofar as they based their very different mystical strengths on the lyrical nature of matter. In a creature as singular as Soutine, who seems to draw only on himself, how are we to discover the influences he really underwent during his preparatory period? They depend more on a vague impregnation than on deliberate orientation. Apart from Cubism, which he resolutely ignored as being contrary to his line, he absorbed, at least by osmosis, a little of all the movements that came after Impressionism. He admired Cézanne and, as with many of his compatriots, declared his predilection for Bonnard. He sometimes mentioned Ensor, Vlaminck, or Kokoschka, but it was above all among the Old Masters that he sought support or confirmation. He examined Tintoretto, El Greco, Rembrandt, Corot, Courbet. The French tradition, with its reconciliation of formal harmony and pungent matter, held his attention. He longed for the rich fullness of the Primitives. In his studio he had a reproduction of the *Portrait of Charles VII* by Fouquet, one of his favorite paintings, in which majesty of composition does nothing to impair the profoundly truthful expression. Was it not the same thing that he achieved in his turn, using very personal means, in the admirable *Portrait of the Sculptor Miestchaninoff*, in which the painter's friend is explored to the point of caricature, then invested with royal grandeur?

After he had painted this masterpiece, in 1923, he returned to Cagnes in less difficult material circumstances. He then wrote to Zborowski—he, Soutine, who never unburdened himself—a let-

ter that must be reproduced in full, for it sheds light on his creative neurosis, reveals his anguish and instability, his complete dependence on environment, and his own mood:

> I received the money order. Thank you. I'm sorry I didn't write to you sooner about my work. It's the first time I haven't been able to do anything. I'm in a bad state of mind and demoralized and that affects me.

> I've only seven canvases. I'm sorry. I'd like to leave Cagnes; I can't stand the landscape. I even went for a few days to Cap Martin, for I thought of settling there. I didn't like it. So I'm back in Cagnes against my will and instead of landscapes I'm going to have to do some wretched still lifes. You can imagine what an undecided state I'm in. Couldn't you suggest some place, for several times I've been on the point of returning to Paris?

Jewish and, if we are to judge from his flat face and Mongol features, perhaps Tartar too, definitely the descendant of wandering peoples, Soutine spent his whole life moving house, changing studios, coming and going between Paris and the country, searching for the propitious time and place, the shock of inspiration that would startle him out of his natural lethargy and push him into painting a canvas. For he could only paint during these dazzling moments of hallucination, of total communion with the theme, when the visible reveals the invisible essence that it embodies metaphorically. His cry of distress from Cagnes—as Monroe Wheeler stresses in his excellent monograph—came immediately before one of the highest points in Soutine's career. He never painted better than in the old Provençal village he thought he could no longer stand. The tempestuous style of the Céret days gave way to austere, airy, finely articulated visions. One of these landscapes—perhaps the closest to perfection in the artist's output, steeped in the ineffable tenderness of the tragic painter—breathes oriental grace beneath the subtle tracery of its surface (Plate VII). Fairylike tones of blue, green, yellow, and red stand out against the shimmering, milky whites of which Soutine alone knew the secret. He drew the richest variations from them in the series of *Pastrycooks* executed between 1922 and 1927, and in the frothy dress, spreading over the entire canvas, of his extraordinary *The Communicant* (Plate X), technically rivaling Watteau's *Gilles*.

His new, easy, sumptuous touch spreads forth in the magnificent still lifes of *Fish and Tomatoes* (Plate VI) contrasting with the starved still lifes of the earlier days. The forks sometimes persist (page 23), but their grip is looser, and aggressiveness is transformed into flamboyant sensuality.

In 1925 Soutine was living in a fairly huge studio in the rue du Mont-Saint-Gothard, where he painted the formidable series, *Carcasses of Beef*, in circumstances that have become legendary. When the whole carcasses that he had delivered still steaming from the slaughterhouses began to dry up, he sent Paulette Jourdain, the girl Zborowski had put at his disposition, to fetch fresh blood from the butcher's to sprinkle over them. The smell bothered the neighbors so much that they called the police, but not before he had had time to paint at least the three monumental versions that now hang in the museums of Amsterdam, Grenoble, and Buffalo (Plate XIII). The crimsons that radiate over midnight blue backgrounds and the splendor of the entrails swell

Drawing, Figure III (Collection M. et Mme Castaing, Paris)

to cosmic proportions. Inspired by Rembrandt, treated in the abrupt manner of Géricault and Goya, the consubstantial theme of Soutine's pictorial genius shakes us to the core, for without romanticism he brings us face to face with the tragic mystery and phosphorescent presence of death in the midst of life.

As a child—and the impression was indelibly printed in his very marrow in a mixture of attraction and horror—Soutine had seen the village *shochet* (ritual slaughterer) killing and bleeding chickens for New Year celebrations and purification rites. So, a shattering series of plucked or half-plucked poultry runs parallel to the carcasses of beef, in a narrower but sharper register. These birds are not arranged on tables like ordinary still lifes, but hang by the beak or claws against a wall, immolated victims whose cry of agony tears their throats. What force stronger than sadism spurred Soutine to multiply these dramatic images which are also, for his painterly eye, ineffable delights? In his seminal essay from 1929, Elie Faure commented memorably:

> It is in flesh already dead that he finds his sensual joy. But this flesh must have bled, we must still see red tears welling up in the place of the wrenched-out feathers, doubtful patches must show through the gold of the skin, the green or blue gems that remain of the wings must be stained with sticky crimson. He hangs his birds by the neck, beaks open, eyes and tongues sticking out, the marvelous coruscations of crests and wattles still swollen and running with juices stilled forever. Sometimes they are nailed up by the two wings, their necks limp and their warm nakedness spattered with red, and recall some liturgical crucifixion for heaven knows what holocaust in honor of the sacred appetites of the human animal. Cruelty here, which does not stem from the mind, but springs from the heart in obedience to the inexorable forces that bind us to the necessity of death.

This in no way excluded pity, for each of us is at once victim and executioner, this cruelty of the *onlooker* who examines the evidence and reveals the fatal inevitability of universal murder is also, in Soutine's case, the reverse form of love and mystic communion. Finally, in what Jean Révol aptly calls his " tortured matter " that exalts the corruption of death, did he not find his rarest, most solemn harmonies, his Baudelairean flowers of evil?

Soutine was an enthusiastic and regular visitor of museums. One of the paintings in front of which he lingered most happily, right from his first days in Paris, was Courbet's *Funeral at Ornans,* a prodigiously executed work that stupefies every painter and was considered by Marquet to be the greatest marvel of The Louvre. Set down with a majestic, stiff hand, a whole village stands assembled on its own ground, in its own local costumes, its own ultimate truth. Soutine was struck most of all by the centers of light in the composition, the fantastic red-robed beadles and the choirboys in white surplices: these may lie at the origin of the *Choirboys* that he himself painted from 1925 to 1930, full length, half-length or bust, in profile or three-quarters, standing or sitting, with or without surplices. The clumsily worn ecclesiastical vestments accentuate, by contrast, the sickly or awkward appearance of the models, and offset splendidly on green or bluish grounds the two sovereign colors of his palette, flesh tones and whites. After all, his earliest still lifes were, significantly enough, *Lilies* and *Lilacs.* What words could do justice to the freshness of his whites, more subtle than those of Utrillo, and the triumphal variety of his reds, crimsons, and carmines, and maroons? They are the flux of ardor and revolt, the substance of fire itself, of blood.

> *Un sang rouge et vivant, dont la toile s'abreuve*
> *Avec l'avidité d'un pré*
> (A live red blood, drunk up by the canvas
> Thirsty as a meadow)

and the reds of Soutine explode, culminating in 1927 with the *Pageboys* and *Doormen*, famous specimens of which are now in the Rothschild collection and the museums of Paris and Buffalo. They are shown in full face, sometimes resigned, sometimes provocative. An immense, disarticulate marionette, his hand stretched out for the tip he covets with all his being, the *Pageboy at Maxim's* (Plate XIV) is one of the most virulent figures in modern art. There is, however, neither satire nor " message " in these implacable observations that continue the work of Lautrec in exploring a neglected sector of mankind. Soutine, unlike the Fauves, never exaggerated his colors solely for their decorative resonance. However strongly they burst out, they are always steeped in human richness and expressive aptness. " What are colors," asked Hugo von Hofmannsthal, " if they do not reveal the innermost life of objects? "

Sprung forth in its own aura of light at the same time as the carcasses of beef, the first *Choirboy* (Plate VIII) is a vibrant outpouring of color itself. Shortly after its rendering, for that is indeed the word, Marcellin and Madeleine Castaing bought it for thirty thousand francs, a considerable sum of money at that time, and far above the highest current prices. Better still, they did not hesitate to dispose of an already remarkable modern collection in order to devote themselves exclusively to their chosen painter, whose burning light eclipsed all others in their eyes. Soutine then agreed to meet these curious collectors, an initial interview with whom a few years before had come to an abrupt end, through his own fault: in the depths of poverty, with his untamed pride, he had feared they were acting out of charity. Now with prosperity, he was seized by the opposite fear, that his canvases were perhaps sought after purely for reasons of speculation. In summer 1929, during a health cure at Châtel-Guyon, confidence grew up between the mistrustful bohemian and this middle-class couple, who were sufficiently clear-sighted and independent-minded to recognize the artist's genius and accept the singular aspects of the man. In an increasingly supple and profound flow of work, Soutine was to paint several portraits of *Madeleine Castaing* (Plate XVIII) and one of *Maria Lani* (Plate XIX), but his usual models remained household staff, servants in kitchen aprons (Plate XV), and liveried domestics. Daumier, Degas, Lautrec, all the great modern analysts had turned their attention to people of inferior condition, trapped in a situation or a trade, the disinherited and declassed who had held an equal fascination for Velázquez and the other Spanish masters. Soutine, whose psychological approach is still more troubled and harsh, spontaneously joined the brotherly universe of Dostoevsky's *The Insulted and the Injured.*

Fame and prosperity could not ease his anguish or change his behavior. The ever-increasing demands of his work, absolute submission to his inner dæmon, his personal morality, were his only reasons for living. From 1930 till the outbreak of war, he stayed long and regularly at Lèves, near Chartres, in the astonishing house that Madeleine Castaing had transformed into a poetic creation, a fairyland straight from the pages of Nerval. He loved the park with its mysterious corners, the adjoining farm where he watched the animals his brushes were to put down with primitive naïveté, the views opening onto town or country; he became attached to the estate, which revived his imagination and is still filled with his presence. In his dark wanderings he found a haven of peace and understanding there, the regenerating atmosphere necessary for his undermined health. Without sacrificing his independence or his savage nature—he would hide during receptions or visits—he felt a naïve joy at being admitted into a cultivated home, penetrating inside French ways and culture. He read Balzac, Michelet, the poets, and he, who already possessed all the knowledge of the initiated, tried with touching sincerity to start from scratch on his missing education. Among the strange guests at Lèves there had been the composer Erik Satie and, in Soutine's time, the memorialist Maurice Sachs, who sometimes evoked the atmosphere of the place in his articles. In a resounding piece in the *Nouvelle Revue Française* in 1934, the latter celebrated Soutine by demolishing all other artists except Utrillo. " The two times I saw Soutine," he recalled in *Le Sabbat*, " I was moved by his soft, wild gaze ... he was noble and at the same time had the hunted air of some proud, solitary animal horrified by the footsteps of man, but never sacrificing the secret laws or pride of its race ... I found in his canvases a terrible, involuntary distortion, undergone in fear and trembling, that all his efforts aimed at taming."

This, indeed, is the direction of the last period, grandiose and little known, during which he led his passionate exaltation to the point of classical mastery. When the Lèves paintings, only some of which are reproduced in this book, are finally shown, it will be time to complete the truncated history of Soutine's career with the final chapter that will establish the work in its complete perspective and growing importance.

The observations gathered by his attentive patrons during the mature years, when they had the privilege of the first viewing and helped him in his work with as much patience as psychological insight, throw much light on his creative approach and his contradictory emotional states. A predestined painter, Soutine trusted only his instinct and obeyed only the mysterious calls of his vocation. Periods of exhaustion or torpor succeeded fertile trance states in irregular cycles. He spent whole weeks, sometimes months, in sterile relapses, incapable of taking up a brush without being impelled to it by some superior need. He was waiting for the unforeseen shock that would drag him from the somnolence during which he gathered strength in between paroxysms of nervous energy. But when what he himself called " the miracle " suddenly happened, nothing could halt him in his total, wild dash toward the inaccessible that only gives itself up in lightning flashes, and the reality behind the painting that is the only basis for truth.

He followed a complicated ritual, similar to the preparation of material by the mystics, in the choice of the canvas itself—old and already painted, all the better for the painter to graft

Young Polish Girl (Collection Mrs. H. Harris Jonas, New York)

his own energy onto it—of the appropriate model or theme, the most suitable lighting and expression. When he was ready to attack the canvas, all his colors were carefully laid out, each one with a different brush depending on the tint or intensity. Soutine began with forty or so brushes, which he threw to the ground after use; his creative frenzy was so great that one day he dislocated his thumb in action. " It all depends," he said, " on the way you mix color, catch it, place it," and no contemporary painter was more specifically gifted than he in that domain. Whenever possible he dashed off the canvas in a single session, so that each stroke should convey the continuous fire of inspiration. If success did not seem absolute, and it could only be so under these precise conditions, he destroyed implacably. Some of the less scrupulous dealers and collectors have been known to rummage through his garbage cans to reconstitute torn works. Many of his paintings are grouped in obsessional series. They are not formal variations on the same theme, in the Impressionist or Romantic sense, but the anxious, desperate quest for a reality, always complex and different.

He demanded complete, often tyrannical submission from the model expressly chosen for each figure. Marcellin Castaing has told of the circumstances which gave *Woman Reading* (Plate XXXVI) its intensity of expression. The situation surrounding the execution of *Woman Wading* (Plate XXIII) is no less dramatic and astonishing. For the position and spiritual atmosphere, Soutine took his inspiration from Rembrandt's *Woman in Her Bath*, the London panel even more radiantly intimate than the contemporary *Bathsheba* in The Louvre. Even in such a case as this he needed a model, and naturally this proved difficult to find. After much prospecting in the area round Chartres, he finally chose a humble peasant girl embodying at once the entire species and the particular effect desired. He had first to overcome her reticence and allay her husband's suspicions. At last she consented to strike the exact pose in which she is shown, under the arch of a bridge, lifting her skirt and standing up to her knees in the stream that flows through the park at Lèves. It is a bewitchingly poetic spot. Soutine was painting away one summer evening when a storm broke. He went on in the pelting rain, lit by flashes of lightning, drenched to the skin, and unaffected by the terrified screams of the model. The result is a masterpiece of majestic splendor, the most touching homage to the modesty and dignity of woman clothed in her perishable, trembling flesh: a supreme monument. Apart from this exceptional canvas with its incomparable chromatic density, there is only one *Nude* (Plate XXX) by Soutine, a studio work on a black ground, strangely lit. The half-length model is obviously astonished by her disturbing effect on the painter, shown through the broad, distracted, though intransigently truthful execution.

Soutine declared boundless admiration for Rembrandt. He often went to Amsterdam to sink in contemplation of *The Jewish Bride*, in which he found what Van Gogh called " the superhuman infinite, half glimpsed," in which the richest color is spiritual illumination. In the more sensual naïveté of Courbet he found the same religious ability to animate the pictorial surface and convey the fullness of life. In Lèves he made an excellent variation on the *Girls Beside the Seine*, and several animal studies inspired by the master of Ornans, including *The Salmon* (Plate XXXIII) and *The Little Calf* (Plate XXXII). Reduction to a smaller scale gives these marvels of cruel or ingenuous observation the precious quality of miniatures, while Soutine resumes the tonal practices of his predecessor in the lively scintillation of colors or their delicate radiance. We have to go back to Giotto to find a more naturally portrayed *Donkey* (Plate XXXI) and the milky modulation of the blues and greens is a chromatic success as difficult to achieve as the result is exquisite.

While he stayed at Lèves, Soutine was always within sight of Chartres Cathedral, silhouetted against the sky and framed in a gap in the trees of the park. He had developed a passion for the Catholic liturgy and secretly haunted churches during Mass. Following in the footsteps of Corot and Utrillo, but with a fantastic impetus all his own, he in his turn erected the sublime façade, the two asymmetrical spires, all the complicated structure and supreme majesty of the cathedral, against the sky of Beauce (Plate XXVII). The luminous glory that transfigures the interior of the nave with the streaming fire of the stained-glass windows overflows outside and penetrates into the substance of the stone, tempered by the soft air. A bright pinkish-brown outline and strong accents of red and black sustain the shimmering opal blues and melting shades of green. Soutine's violently personal mysticism here echoes the collective faith of the Middle Ages, still animated by an oriental feeling for colors and their divine equivalencies. He painted many versions of this illustrious subject in 1933. In the following year Soutine concentrated his chromatic fervor on a more humble vehicle: the *House at Oisème* (Plate XXIX), an old dwelling set among trees, drawing its mystery from its own hallucinating reality. A synthesis of Cézanne and Courbet in some ways, this is one of the finest landscapes ever painted, saturated with the strange luminosity peculiar to Soutine, which lays bare the innermost essence of the place.

In 1937 Soutine moved into Villa Seurat, in the Alésia district of Paris. One of his neighbors there was his compatriot Chana Orloff, who sometimes invited him to her house, and one day discovered that he had learned by heart, for his own pleasure, the works of Pushkin, one of the world's greatest voices, and that he was similarly enchanted by the music of Bach. After an obscure, highly complicated, sentimental life, he finally accepted the presence in his studio of a " red-haired model " of German origins, Gerda Groth, whom he immediately renamed Mademoiselle Garde. She went with him on his furtive outings and to his favorite distractions, boxing matches and the cinema. Soutine was fascinated by boxing matches and their implacable rigor. Through some deep-rooted association of ideas in his metaphorically-inclined mind, he saw them as manifestations in action of the antique statues he was growing to admire more and more exclusively in The Louvre, and whose perfection was his aim, to be achieved through the specific language of color conceived in terms of more than decoration. If one looks attentively at his work, and forgets the habitual clichés, nothing in contemporary art better evokes archaic Grecian sculpture than these last paintings of figures from 1930 on, when he achieved classical balance and went beyond his initial expressionism. Think of the dense plastic sense, the vibrant precision in the faces of *Charlot* (Plate XXIV) and Jeanne (Plate XXV), and the admirable *Woman's Profile* (Plate XXXV). Daumier's inner strength and Lautrec's vivacity join forces abruptly in these works. Form and character spring from the same painterly flow, diversified with as much exactitude as splendor.

In summer 1939, war overtook Soutine and his mistress in Civry, a little village in the *département* of the Yonne, near Avallon. During this time of stress he painted shattered landscapes, *Windy Day, Auxerre* (Plate XL) and *Return from School After the Storm* (Plate XLI), crossed by the figures of two children, running and holding each other by the hand, marvelously drawn against the stormy expanse of the canvas. Like Van Gogh at Auvers-sur-Oise, Soutine, an exile in the country he had made his own, revived his own earliest memories at the end of his wanderings.

All witnesses and biographers admit that Soutine never made drawings, except perhaps the occasional rapid preparatory sketch in charcoal. In fact he was incapable of controlling or channeling the surge of his inspiration and, following the example of the greatest virtuosi, Hals and Velázquez, always attacked the canvas directly with color. The only drawings of his that have been preserved, freely executed as such in their own right and not merely preparatory sketches, which have remained unknown for years and are reproduced here for the first time, date from this troubled period he spent in Civry. They are exclusively devoted to faces, rising like apparitions in a whirlwind of lines and spirals radiating around the mouths and eyes. Stumbling clumsiness or inspired sureness? The most striking aspect, which shows Soutine's fundamental attitude to painting, is the absence of any indication of space, of any learned convention: the pinning down in the very moment, of life in its depth and continuity. One rarely sees an equivalent to this graphic intensity outside the German Primitives from Grünewald to Dürer.

In May 1940, Gerda Groth was sent to a concentration camp because of her nationality. Soutine stayed on in Civry until February 1941. Then, when persecution of the Jews began, he hid for some months in Paris, before finding a refuge in Touraine, at Champigny-sur-Veuldre near Chinon. He settled there with another companion, Marie-Berthe Aurenche, an ex-wife of Max Ernst. In spite of his difficult financial situation and his ruined health, he never stopped painting his favorite subjects: animals, children, trees. The tree cult, which survived until very late in the Germanic and Slavic countries, belongs to the most universal and primitive mythology. At the end of the last century the Lithuanian peasants in the Smilovichi region still laid offerings at the foot of the finest specimens in the rich forest that surrounded their villages. Did a memory of these ancient rites have anything to do with the almost religious homage Soutine bestowed upon trees? In 1929 he painted several luxuriant versions of the famous *Tree of Vence* (Plates XX, XXI), the giant ash tree with its trunk held in by iron rings, that stands looming over the houses that curve around the square at the entrance to the old town. A little later, in Chartres, where the cathedral itself is a forest, tall vaults of foliage were to rear their great leafy arches in the vibrant, luminous air. But most of all it was in the country around Civry and Champigny that he produced, during the last months of his life, a wealth of treescapes in which we see tiny, astonishing animals and rustic figures setting the scale. Branching out in space, immemorially ancient, the tree is the ideal symbol of the cosmic system and the inexhaustible image of the renewal of life. It participates in all the elements, marks the rhythmic passing of the seasons, quivers at the slightest atmospheric change. Soutine represents them sometimes as isolated giants, spreading out their vast wreaths to swallow up the tumult of the winds (Plate XLII), sometimes as tall, solid masses that weave supple networks of branches against the delicate, milky sky (Plates XLIII, XLIV). His headstrong lyricism settles and broadens in bowing, in these last master-pieces, before the waves of space and light, giving subtle shades, according to the time and the winds, to the infinite variations of this vegetable-flesh placed beyond human passions and pene-trated, from the deepest roots to the last twig, by the universal flow of life. On a dominant register of blues and greens broken with whites, in place of the reds of the past, color is led to its supplest flowering, a perfect fusion of the artist's soul and the life-sap of nature. The breath of the visionary is inseparable from the realistic fidelity vowed to the nature of the land. " That really is our country! " exclaimed some peasants who surprised Soutine at work one day, and this remark touched him more than all the praise of experts.

Like Corot, whose figures he had appreciated, or Renoir or Bonnard, Soutine excelled in conveying the innocence of children (Plates XXXVII, XLV). Lastly the medieval theme of *Mother and Child*, linked to each other like the human tree of life, reappears periodically in his work (Plate XXXIX) and culminates in a staggering *Motherhood* (Plate XXXVIII).

Soutine died in Paris on August 9, 1943, after an operation—too late—for the stomach ulcer that had been tormenting him for years. Matisse had bought one of his canvases and Picasso, defying the rules of the Occupation, followed his funeral cortège to the Montparnasse cemetery.

PLATES

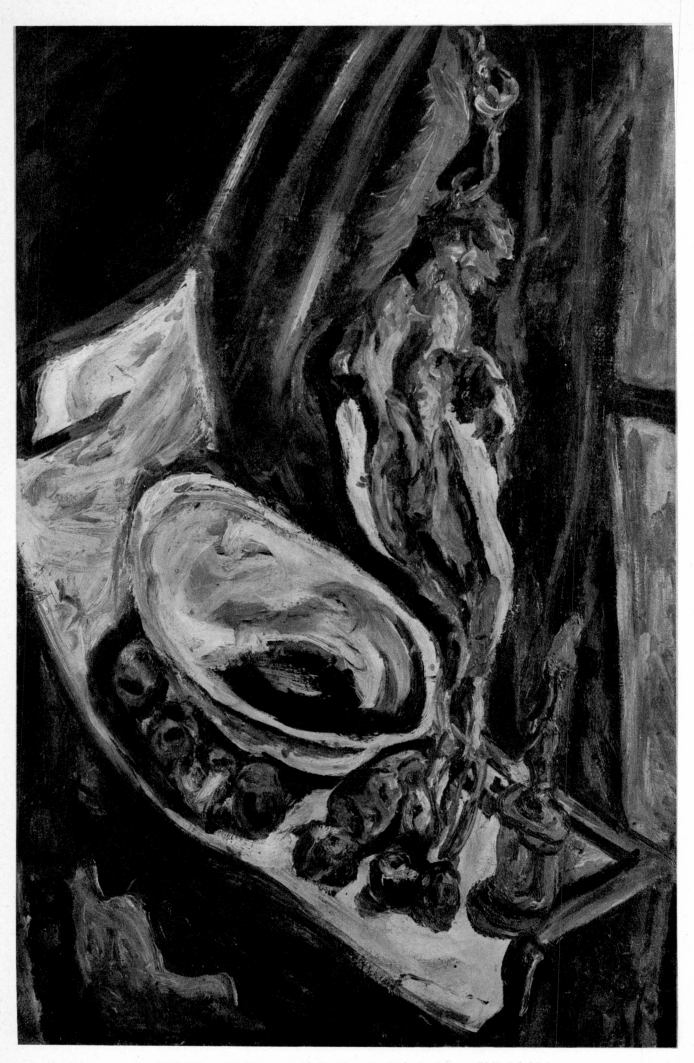

I - *Still Life with Pheasant* (Collection Frederic R. Mann, Philadelphia)

II - *Herrings and Bottle* (Collection M. et Mme Castaing, Paris)

III - *Farm Girl* (Collection Dr. and Mrs. Harry Bakwin, New York)

IV - *Woman in Red* (Collection Dr. and Mrs. Harry Bakwin, New York)

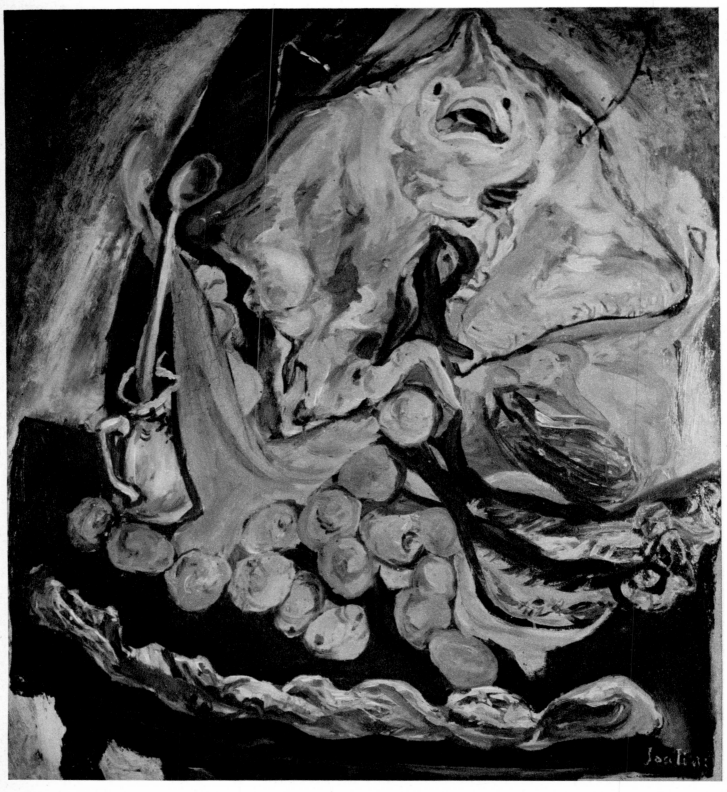

V - *Ray-Fish with Bread* (Collection François Reichenbach)

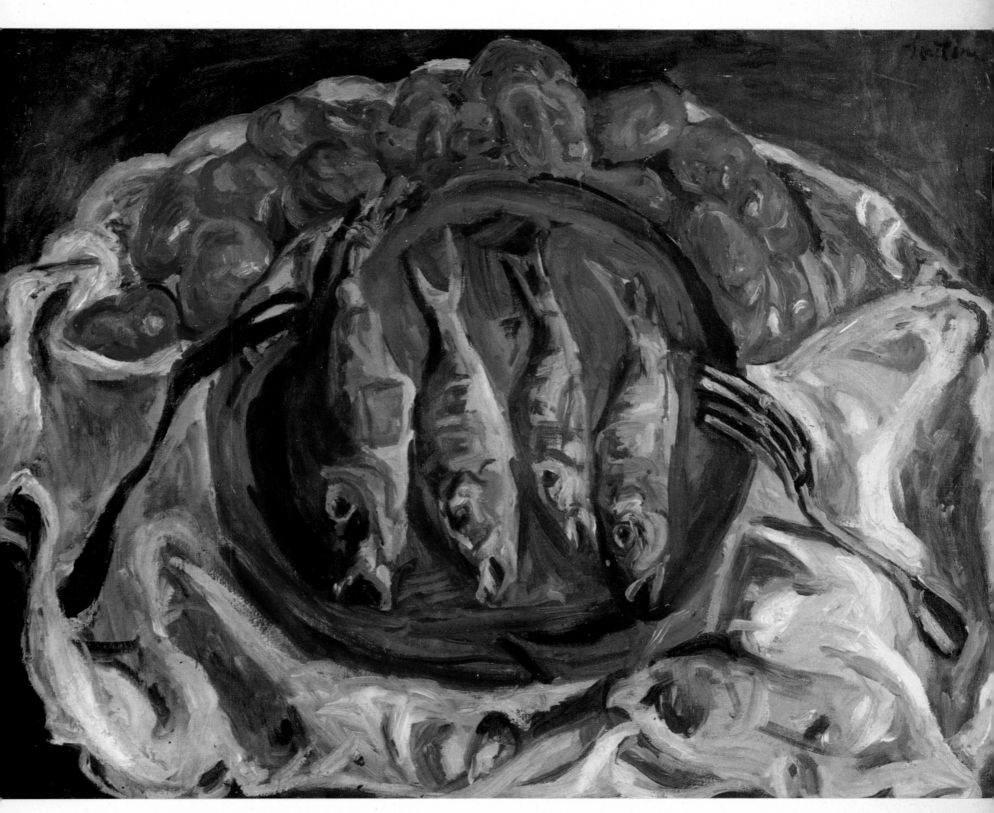

VI - *Fish and Tomatoes* (Collection Mr. and Mrs. Jack I. Poses, New York)

VII - *Landscape, Cagnes* (Collection M. et Mme Castaing, Paris)

VIII - *Choirboy* (Collection M. et Mme Castaing, Paris)

IX - *Choirboy with Surplice* (Collection Mme Jean Walter, Paris)

X - *The Communicant* (Collection Mr. Edward G. Robinson, Beverly Hills)

XI - *The Pastrycook* (Collection Mr. and Mrs. Lee A. Ault, New York)

XII - *Rembrandt: Flayed Ox* (The Louvre, Paris)

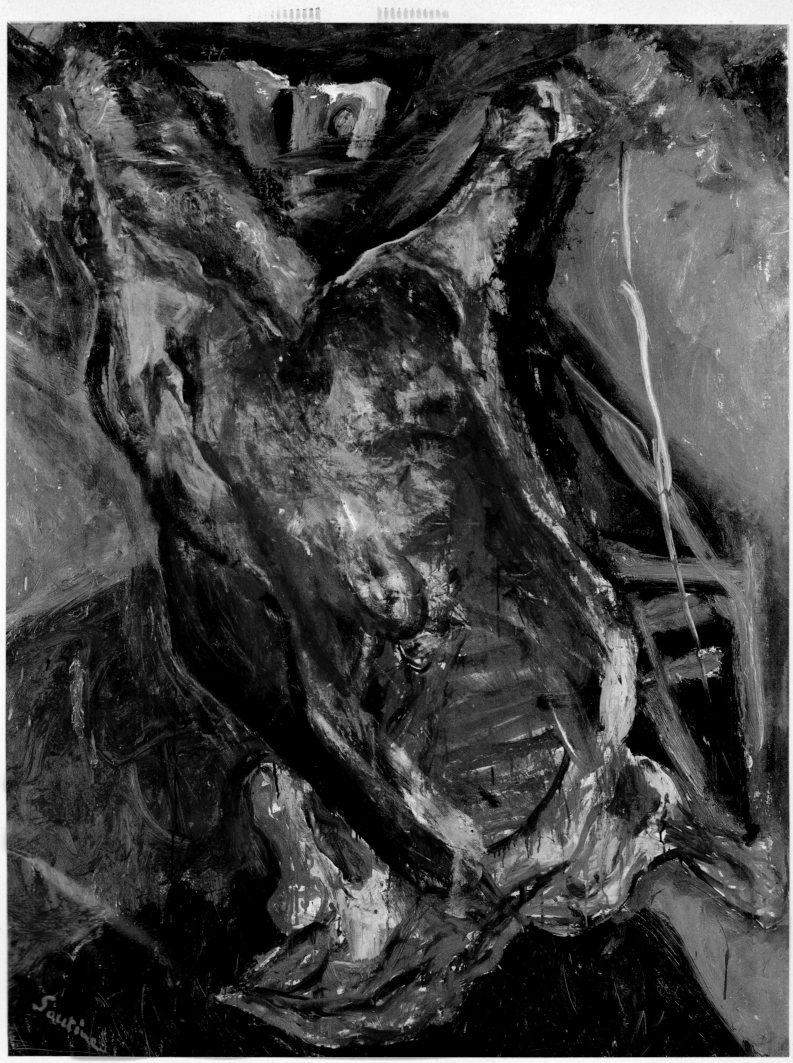

XIII - *Carcass of Beef* (The Albright-Knox Art Gallery, Buffalo)

XIV - *Page Boy at Maxim's* (The Albright-Knox Art Gallery, Buffalo)

XV - *The Cook* (Collection Mr. and Mrs. Leigh B. Block, Chicago)

XVI - *The Valet* (Collection Mr. and Mrs. Leigh B. Block, Chicago)

XVII - *Portrait of Boy in Blue* (Collection Mr. and Mrs. Ralph F. Colin, New York)

XVIII - *Portrait of Madeleine Castaing* (The Metropolitan Museum of Art, New York)

XIX - *Portrait of Maria Lani* (The Museum of Modern Art, New York [Sam A. Lewisohn Bequest])

XX - *Tree of Vence* (Collection M. et Mme Castaing, Paris)

XXI - *Tree of Vence* (Collection Mrs. Lloyd Bruce Wescott, Rosemont, New Jersey)

XXII - *Woman Bathing* (Collection M. et Mme Castaing, Paris)

XXIII - *Woman Wading* (Collection M. et Mme Castaing, Paris)

XXIV - *Portrait of Charlot* (Collection M. et Mme Castaing, Paris)

XXV - *Portrait of a Girl* (Collection M. et Mme Castaing, Paris)

XXVI - *Corot: Chartres Cathedral* (The Louvre, Paris)

XXVII - *Chartres Cathedral* (Collection Mrs. Lloyd Bruce Wescott, Rosemont, New Jersey)

XXVIII - *Alley of Trees (Les Grands Prés)* (Collection M. et Mme Castaing, Paris)

XXIX - *House at Oisème* (Collection Mr. Richards H. Emerson, Lakeville, Conn.)

XXX - *Female Nude* (Collection Mr. and Mrs. Ralph F. Colin, New York)

XXXI - *The Donkey* (Collection M. et Mme Castaing, Paris)

XXXII - *The Little Calf* (Collection M. et Mme Castaing, Paris)

XXXIII - *The Salmon*. Oil on wood (Collection Mr. and Mrs. Ralph F. Colin, New York)

XXXIV - *Reclining Woman* (Collection M. et Mme Castaing, Paris)

XXXV - *Woman's Profile* (The Phillips Collection, Washington, D.C.)

XXXVI - *Woman Reading* (Collection M. et Mme Castaing, Paris)

XXXVII - *Seated Child in Blue* (Collection M. et Mme Castaing, Paris)

XXXVIII - *Motherhood* (Collection M. et Mme Castaing, Paris)

XXXIX - *Mother and Child* (Collection M. et Mme Castaing, Paris)

XL - *Windy Day, Auxerre* (The Phillips Collection, Washington, D.C.)

XLI - *Return from School After the Storm* (The Phillips Collection, Washington D.C.)

XLII - *Wind-blown Tree* (Collection M. et Mme Castaing, Paris)

XLIII - *After the Storm* (Collection M. et Mme Castaing, Paris)

XLIV - *Autumn Trees, Champigny* (Collection M. et Mme Castaing, Paris)

XLV - *Child in Red* (Collection M. et Mme Castaing, Paris)

EXHIBITIONS OF SOUTINE'S WORKS

1927 Paris, Galerie Bing, June.

1935 Chicago, Arts Club, December 13—30.

1936 New York, Valentine Gallery, February 3—22.
New York, Mrs. Cornelius J. Sullivan Gallery, February 24—March 15.

1937 New York, Mrs. Cornelius J. Sullivan Gallery, March 22—April 17.
New York, Valentine Gallery, May 3—22.
London, Leicester Galleries, April (Preface by Maurice Sachs).

1939 New York, Valentine Gallery, March 20—April 18.

1940 New York, Carroll Carstairs Gallery, April 15—May 11 (Preface by Henry McBride).

1943 Washington, D.C., The Phillips Collection, January 17—February 15 (Preface by Duncan Phillips).
New York, Bignou Gallery, March 22—April 16 (Preface by Albert C. Barnes).

1944 New York, Niveau Gallery, October 7—November 2 (Preface by M. Georges-Michel).

1945 Paris, Galerie de France, January 12—February 28 (Preface by L. Parrot).

1947 London, Gimpel Fils, April 23—May 17 (Preface by M. Collis).
Paris, Galerie Zak, November 29—December 31

1950—51 New York, The Museum of Modern Art, October 31—January 7; The Cleveland Museum of Art, January 30—March 18 (Catalogue by Monroe Wheeler).

1952 Venice, Biennale (Preface by J. Leymarie).

1956 Paris, Maison de la Pensée Française, March—April.

1959 Paris, Galerie Charpentier (Preface by W. George and M. Castaing).

1963 Edinburgh, Royal Scottish Academy, August 17—September 15; London, Tate Gallery, September 28—November 3 (Preface by David Sylvester).

BIOGRAPHICAL SKETCH

1893 Born in Smilovichi, near Minsk, in Lithuania

1907 Leaves his family and goes to Minsk, takes classes in drawing, earning his living retouching for a photographer

1910 Attends art school in Vilna

1913 Arrives in Paris. Studies in Atelier Cormon; settles in Montparnasse, in La Ruche, the cooperative artists' colony, where he finds his friends, Kikoine and Kremègne

1915—17 Cité Falguière; makes acquaintance of Lipchitz, Modigliani, and the dealer Zborowski

1918 First trip to Provence

1919—22 Lives in Céret in the Pyrenees, and Cagnes in the Alpes Maritimes. Tragic period culminating in the death of Modigliani; returns to Paris in late 1922; massive purchase of his works, by the famous American collector, Dr. Albert C. Barnes

1925 Paris, studio rue du Mont-Saint-Gothard; paints series, *Carcasses of Beef*

1926 Paris, rue de l'Aude

1927—29 Paris, avenue du Parc de Montsouris. Stays in the Indre, Blanc, Provence, and Châtel-Guyon; paints series of *Pageboys* and *Valets*

1930—35 Paris, passage d'Enfer; travels widely in France; regularly spends summer on the Castaing estate at Lèves, near Chartres

1936 Paris, avenue d'Orléans

1937—39 Paris, Villa Seurat; affair with Gerda Groth, whom he calls Mlle Garde; war finds them in the little village of Civry, near Avallon, in the Yonne

1940 Mlle Garde deported (May 15); Soutine stays on in Civry until February 1941

1941 As a Jew, Soutine is in danger, and hides for some time in Paris, then takes refuge in Champigny-sur-Veuldre, a small village in Touraine, with his mistress Marie-Berthe Aurenche; paints *Landscapes*

1943 Hospitalized with intestinal perforation; operation too late; dies early on August 9. Picasso follows his funeral cortège

BIBLIOGRAPHY

1923 GUILLAUME, P. "Soutine," *Les Arts à Paris*, January.

1924 BARNES, A.C. "Soutine," *Les Arts à Paris*, November.

1926 GEORGE, W. "Soutine," *L'Amour de l'Art*, Paris, November.

1927 CHARENSOL, G. "Soutine," *L'Art Vivant*, Paris, No. 3.

1928 FAURE, E. *Soutine*. Paris.

1930 DRIEU LA ROCHELLE, P. "Soutine," *Formes*, Paris, May.

1932 SACHS, M. "Soutine," *Creative Art*, New York, December.

1934 SACHS, M. "Contre les peintres d'aujourd'hui," *Nouvelle Revue Française*, Paris, July.

1944 SEROUYA, H. "Soutine," *Les Lettres Françaises*, Paris, December 2.

1945 BAZIN, G. "Chaïm Soutine," *Labyrinthe*, Geneva, No. 6.
COGNIAT, R. *Soutine*. Paris.
DI SAN LAZZARO, G. "Ricordo di Soutine," *Tre Arti*, Milan, No. 1.

1948 SOBY, J.T. "Two Painters of Tragedy: Rouault and Soutine," *Contemporary Painters* (The Museum of Modern Art Exhibition Catalogue), New York.

1950 TWORKOV, J. "Wandering Soutine," *Art News*, New York, November.
WHEELER, M. *Soutine*. Museum of Modern Art, New York.

1951 ORLOFF, C. "Mon ami Soutine," *Preuves*, Paris, November.

1952 COGNIAT, R. *Soutine*. Skira, Geneva.

1954 LASSAIGNE, J. *Soutine*. Paris.

1955 SZITTYA, E. *Soutine et Son Temps*. Bibliothèque des Arts, Paris.

1956 Groth, G. (Mlle Garde). "Mes années chez Soutine" (interview with MICHEL RAGON), *L'Œil*, Paris, January

1959 GÉRALDY, P. "Chaïm Soutine ou 'l'enfant manqué,'" *Le Figaro*, Paris, June 25.
RÉVOL, J. "Soutine, matières suppliciées," *Nouvelle Revue Française*, Paris, August.

1961 GREENBERG, C. "Soutine," *Art and Culture*, Boston.
SPERBER, M. "Sur l'art juif," *L'Arche*, Paris, August—September.

TRANSLATED BY JOHN ROSS